MIAMI PROPS

AUSTIN J BROWN & MARK R WAGNER

Osprey Colour Series

Published in 1988 by Osprey Publishing Limited
27A Floral Street, London WC2E 9DP
Member company of the George Philip Group

© Austin J Brown and Mark R Wagner

British Library Cataloguing in Publication Data

Brown, Austin J
  Miami props.—(Osprey colour series)
  1. Transport aeroplanes
  I. Title   II. Wagner, Mark R
  623.74 '65

ISBN 0-85045-883-8

Editor Dennis Baldry
Designed by Paul Kime
Printed in Hong Kong

Front cover Tender is the night as a Trans-Air-Link DC-6 is prepared for a nightime departure from Miami International Airport. Interestingly, the Trans-Air-Link fleet use the call sign 'Skytruck', which is the title of two books by the late Stephen Piercey in the Osprey Colour Series

Title pages A Trans-Air-Link DC-6, full flap lowered, adopts the classic nosedown attitude of the 'Six' during its final descent onto Runway 9 Left at MIA

Back cover Trans-Air-Link's DC-7CF seen through the eye of a cowling

Parked on Trans-Air-Link's apron, this DC-6A sits surrounded by the nose and tail of N3982Y and XA-GAJ respectively. TAL plans to cannibalize one of the 440s to keep the other airworthy

Contents

For Annette and Fiona.

Shortly after our first book, *BIG PROPS*, was published by Osprey in November 1987, we were commissioned to shoot this follow up. Miami is surely the Mecca for those who admire the classic piston-engined transports of yesteryear, its geographical position (with its Caribbean and Latin American connections) ensuring a healthy supply of tired iron. Sequencing the slower 'old ladies' in amongst today's jetliners must pose a significant air traffic problem, but it does not seem to be apparent amid the daily hustle at Miami. Only the availability of aviation gasoline (avgas), or its price, would restrict their operations. As there seems to be no threat in either direction at present within the United States, these wonderful aircraft are destined to survive in steadily decreasing numbers until, and quite possibly beyond, the year 2000.

The picture mix in *MIAMI PROPS* reflects the overall scene at 'Propsville USA'—that's why the editor decided to use the photograph of Angela (right) instead of a boring shot of your intrepid authors! Until the phone call comes through from Hollywood, Angela will continue to sell her delicious hot dogs on the perimeter of Miami International.

MIAMI PROPS was shot on location between 23 February and 23 March 1988 using Nikon cameras loaded with Kodachrome K64.

Austin J Brown and Mark R Wagner
Bristol, April 1988

Heartfelt thanks go to Peter Joel of Pan Am public relations in London
Gary Balnicki of Trans-Air-Link in Miami
Bruce Drum of Dade County Aviation Department and his wife
Pauline and the Aerogem guys
Ron Gardner and Walter Houghton of Broward County Aviation Department at Fort Lauderdale
The whole team at Chalks base at Lauderdale
Jean Bozzuto, press officer of the Virgin Islands Port Authority at St Thomas
And last but not least Glenn 'Herky' Richardson of Rich Photo in Miami who saved the day when we ran out of film (yet again!)

Bellomy Lawson

Climbing into the evening sun, APA's DC-6 retracts the gear as it climbs out against a backdrop of Continental Airlines' jets at the main terminal

Overleaf Following the DC-6 in a motordive sequence, N95BL cleans up abeam the photographer. Based in Santo Domingo, APA lease this aircraft from Bellomy Lawson and it spends most of its time operating out of Miami

Overleaf, inset Back on the ground again, N95BL undergoes a routine check in the open air on the Bellomy Lawson ramp

These pages After landing on 27 Right, DC-6BF N94BL turns off the runway towards the Customs & Immigration building on the north side of the airport. Bellomy Lawson paint the spinners of their fleet in yellow to identify their aircraft from those of other DC-6 operators

Overleaf Bellomy Lawson lease this 1952 vintage DC-6BF, N1304S, to Turks Air, a Miami-based company

Eastern Express

N38PB, now resplendent in Eastern Express colours, operated into Miami for years sporting the Provincetown-Boston logo until their recent takeover by Texas Air Corporation

Overleaf Eastern Express' DC-3A on finals to land on the cross runway

Overleaf, inset N34PB reloads with passengers at Key West Airport before departing for Miami

Above With some jetliners for company, N34PB finds a moments peace in the Eastern Airliners' maintenance area

Top right Spanning an era in airliner technology, Arrow Air's stretched DC-8 must have been an unthinkable development when N40PB was built in 1939. The Douglas DC-3 prepares to leave the commuter terminal at Miami International

Right The Eastern Express ramp in the middle of MIA is usually dominated by DC-3s, but the company also utilizes Saab 340s, Beech 1900s and Beech 99s, all of which feed passengers into Eastern's Miami hub

Overleaf, left inset A gaggle of Gooneys wheel and turn on the central ramp

Overleaf, main picture Taxying out towards Runway 27 Left for departure

Overleaf, right inset N36PB lifts its tail into the air on 27 Left as it passes the Pan Am terminal. A touch of left rudder keeps it straight in the light south westerley as the handling pilot 'walks' the rudder until the aircraft attains flying speed

Above Full flap, which looks insignificant compared with modern high-lift wings, is selected, as N34PB aims for the numbers of Runway 30 in the red evening light

Right N35PB sinks onto the runway in the warm early evening sunshine

NOAA

David Turner, a line skipper with NOAA, poses with his copy of *BIG PROPS* in front of one of the agencies' two Miami-based WP-3D Orions. The National Oceanic and Atmospheric Administration also operate a King Air, a Twin Otter and a Bell helicopter

Left The NOAA WP-3s are covered in sensors and probes which record temperature and humidity. The red and white nose probe collects dust at low level over water or, more technically, the boundary layer between the ocean and atmosphere. Lasers are used to study cloud physics and there is a belly mounted 360° black and white weather radar. The tail houses a vertically sweeping height finding radar for cloud studies and a Doppler system is used to pick out particle movements in storms and clouds

Top left There's no truth in the rumour that they do haircuts on board! The 'barber's pole' is an atmospheric dust collection probe

Above The WP-3s have roomy cockpits and operate with a standard flight crew of three, whilst in the cabin during a scientific sortie would be a crew of up to twenty, consisting of about twelve NOAA computer operators and eight meteorological scientists

Tallying the hurricanes it has hunted, N42RF is painted with its adversaries just forward of the port rear door. Having lived through Hurricanes David and Frederick in the Caribbean in 1979, I can only say that this proves the strength of the Orion's airframe and the courage of NOAA's crews

Alongside we find a tally of countries of operation. The NOAA aircraft can be seconded to feasible projects worldwide for scientific research through the US Department of Commerce

Left A general view of the NOAA ramp

Above Sting in the tail of the WP-3D houses Doppler and height finding radar

Trans-Air-Link

The Trans-Air-Link ramp, featuring three DC-6s and their DC-7. That means sixteen engines for maintenance with 208 pistons and jugs and 576 spark plugs. And that's only part of the fleet!

Left TAL's DC-6 N841TA gets off smartly at St Thomas to clear the hill at the upwind end of Runway One Zero en route back to Miami via San Juan

Inset Watch the paintwork! A bare metal TAL DC-6AC and a white TAL DC-6A on the company ramp

Above The cockpit of DC-6 N870TA boasts a recently fitted instrument panel and always operates with the standard three flight crew

Left DC-6, N841TA, back from Saint Thomas, US Virgin Islands

Rear view of DC-6s on the TAL ramp. Left to right: N841TA, N870TA, N779TA

Cowling covers lie like fallen leaves by this Six
as engineers remove the last piece from
number one engine

Overleaf TAL DC-6, N872TA, waits for the
midnight hour when its crew will arrive to fly it
down the Caribbean island chain, picking up
and dropping off various items of cargo as it
goes

40

Top left Ship '872' is towed into position on the TAL ramp for an inspection

Left With an amazing wealth of piston flying experience behind him, from Alaska to the Caribbean and all stops in between, TAL's director of quality control, Bill Winn, now spends most of his time on the ground

Above Well tucked away in a quiet corner of the TAL ramp was this Convair 440, N910RC, which is due to come on line in the near future as the baby of tho fleet

Above Looking very smart and business-like, N872TA receives attention to its nose wheel oleo

Right There's not much about the DC-7 that TAL's 'Pete' doesn't know. As the company maintenance inspector he takes a look over the Seven before its weekly scheduled trip to Kingston, Jamaica. The four Wright R-3350 fuel injected Turbo Compound engines were originally rated at 3400 hp with the old 115/145 octane 'hot' fuel, but with current 100LL avgas only 2800 hp is produced. That knocks at least 30 knots off the cruising speed

Left TAL's DC-7CF loads up with boxes of hatching eggs and a few rolls of textiles as well as a Non Stop Food Processor, a printing machine, electric toaster and a box of Pampers nappies, grossing 127,000 lbs

Above The seven carries around 8000 lbs more than a Six as well as cruising a little faster. The hatching eggs were stacked towards the front to keep the centre of gravity within limits and strapped to the sides of the cabin to prevent the bulk moving backwards and changing the balance of the aircraft. The lighter miscellaneous pieces filled in the space towards the rear

Top left At 2200 rpm and 32 inches of manifold pressure the indicated airspeed is 200 knots at a cruising altitude of 9000 ft, southbound over the Florida Straits. The average rate of climb to 9000 ft was 400 feet per minute

Left Fisheye view of the three man team at the sharp end of the Seven approaching the north Cuban coastline at 9000 ft

Above A captains eye view of the numbers one and two Wright R-3350s. Below is a town somewhere in central Cuba

Overleaf Coasting in over Jamaica from the north, the Kingston runway, distinctively built on a large tract of reclaimed land, can be seen from a long way out. Short finals to land at Kingston: one mile out, height 300 ft, speed around 150 knots, gear is down and locked with three greens indicated, prop pitch is fully fine, mixtures are fully rich and wheel brakes are off. Landing clearance and wind velocity has been passed from ATC, so select full flap and down we go

Above On arrival at the freight ramp one engine is kept running to supply hydraulic pressure to open the cargo doors. The company ladder is then propped against the forward door and the crew venture out into the warm Kingston air. A cargo representative approaches the crew asking them to bring him a television tube next time they come back, and the unloaders group together and ask for their picture to be taken

Top right The flight crew complete the paperwork for the previous sector and later dig into their sandwich boxes whilst relaxing on some spare trolleys. Jamaica Air Freighters handle the unloading of the cargo at Kingston

Right The Trans-Air-Link DC-7CF started life in July 1957 when it was delivered to KLM as a DC-7C (PH-DSI), in fact the KLM name *Zuider Zee* is still visible on the bare metal nose. In the cockpit the original KLM metal warning notices remain riveted to the instrument panels. During August 1962 the DC-7C was converted to a CF freighter and eventually found its way into Biafra between June 1969 and January 1970. By 1972 it was reported as being semi derelict at Salisbury, Rhodesia. The next information available indicates that it was operated by Air Gabon Cargo (1978), then Air Trans Africa (1979) and then the Rhodesia-Zimbabwe air force by 1980. During the early eighties it was owned by Affretair (VP-YTY) after which it was ferried across to Florida (see *SKY TRUCK*) and joined the Trans-Air-Link fleet during 1984

Left The nose of their DC-7 towers over its TAL crew during the three hours turnaround on the Kingston tarmac. Left to right: First Officer Jo Reeves, Captain Billy Bob Neal and Flight Engineer Geno Gentile

Above Fully loaded with yams, cut flowers and clothing by early evening time and ready for the $2\frac{1}{2}$ hour flight back up to Miami to complete its day's work

Dominican operators

Left Operators from the Dominican Republic add cosmopolitan interest to the big prop scene at MIA. Agro Air operates two Boeing C-97G Stratofreighters and a DC-8 on behalf of Aerochago and Aeromar. Here, with full flap extended, HI-468 pitches its nose down on final approach to 27 Left

Short finals, over the fence. A Piedmont F.28 in the background is on approach to Runway 27 Right

Overleaf Just past the 'piano keys', HI-468 flashes past the United ramp

Overleaf, inset Just a foot or so above the runway the Strat almost flares and eventually impresses everyone with an incredibly smooth nosewheel first touchdown

Left Real Agro for dedicated mechanics. One of Agro Air's C-97Gs receives a spot of attention on the southwest ramp at Miami

Above A fairly regular visitor to MIA during the first half of 1988 was HI-515, a Super Constellation operated by Aerolineas Mundo (AMSA). Seen here taxying to the 27 Left holding point loaded with freight bound for the Bahamas

Overleaf A few weeks later HI-515 taxis from the customs and immigration centre on the north side of MIA to the south west ramp to unload its newly arrived cargo

Overleaf, inset As luck would have it the blackest cloud in all Florida passed over as the Connie rolled down 27 Left and departed the zone just about maintaining a positive rate of climb

64

These pages and overleaf Transporte Aereo
Dominicano SA (TRADO) appeared during 1980
operating a L-749 Constellation. Today the
company owns two DC-6s, one of which is
withdrawn from use. HI-454 did not move for
over a month from its position on the Butler
Aviation ramp at MIA; surprisingly it is
supposed to be the active member of the fleet

The smaller companies

Fancy an Air Adventure? Then contact the company at Fort Lauderdale's Hollywood Airport for a whirl in their passenger carrying DC-3

Next to the Air Adventure machine, in the
northeast corner of FTL, was N47CR, another
pretty DC-3. The four chimneys on top of the
fuselage were not a factory fitted option on the
standard model

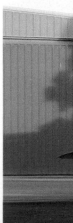

Dakota N92578 was found hiding in the evening shadows at Fort Lauderdale Executive Airport

These pages An ex-Millardair DC-3 recently re-registered as N87664 was parked at Opa Locka Airport next to DC-6 N843TA

Overleaf As one Opa Locka Airport worker exclaimed, 'Everything on this goddam airport is for sale—except me!'

FOR SALE
685-1204
EMERGENCY EXIT

Left Comair operate Bandeirantes from Hollywood Airport, FTL which feed into Delta's system

Above Sedalia-Marshall-Boonville Stageline Inc of Dallas, Texas, own this Convair 600. Converted from a 1948 Convair 240-0, the 600 is powered by two Rolls-Royce Dart 542-4 turboprop engines. N74850 was leased from SMB to a Miami based operator during early 1988 and is one of nearly 20 Dart powered Cv600 and 640s in SMB's fleet

Above Aerolineas El Salvador, SA de CV (known as AESA to the lads), operate this Douglas DC-6BF alongside one other out of San Salvador. YS-05C is seen here at MIA undergoing major maintenance on number one, the prop having been removed

Top right This Martin 4-0-4 spent most of February and March 1988 being worked on and bore no titles. The large roof in the background is the Pan Aviation hangar

Right Sunbird Air, based on the National Jet ramp at FTL, operate two Convair 440s. N411GA wears a dark blue and yellow livery whilst N26DR is red and purple

Overleaf Miami Air Lease operate this ex-Varig C-46 Commando N625CL from MIA's northwest corner to San Juan, Santo Domingo and the Bahamas

Above Cooling out with Syndi-Sue. This group of school kids sunbathed on the tarmac next to their aeroplane while it was rendered serviceable, eventually taking off for the Bahamas a little later than scheduled

Top right A familiar sight on Miamis north side is Transportes Aereos Naciónales (TAN Airlines) Lockheed L-188CF Electra, HR-TNL, which carries freight to and from Honduras

Right Fairchild F.27, N311NA, owned by Air Cortez of California didn't move from its parked position for many weeks at MIA

The Caicos Caribbean Airways DC-6, N43867, on the National Jet ramp at FTL waiting to be worked on before its next mission

Above Douglas DC-4, N74183, parked behind the Caicos Caribbean DC-6 at FTL, where it has been resident since at least the early eighties

Top right A new machine for Aerovias, registered TG-CGO, this DC-6 prepares for loading before its return journey to Guatemala City. The carrier principally operates a fleet of Piper twins and Handley Page Heralds

Right Bare metal rules, OK? A view of the F A Conner ramp in the northwest corner of Miami International, revealing some DC-6s, a Twin Bonanza and a DC-7 tail

Top left An anonymous line up of Twin Beeches (Beech 18s or C-45s) on the Conner ramp. The DC-8 must be one of the first of Conner's fleet to wear any paint

Left N522SJ is a Lockheed L-382E Hercules operated by Southern Air Transport from their heavily guarded and fenced ramp on the northern perimeter of MIA. SAT specializes in the movement of outsize cargo as well as contract and ad hoc freight services for commercial clients, the US and foreign governments, using a mixed fleet of Boeing 707s and Hercules

Above This chance meeting with the rear end of a SAT Boeing 707 flight engineer's old Dodge at the traffic lights on NW 36th Street suggests that the driver is not only socially outgoing, but also a veteran of 'Spectre' Hercules gunship missions during the Vietnam conflict. It is alleged that Southern Air Transport is what used to be called Air America, or 'Air CIA'. SAT's worldwide trucking capabilities are graphically described by the company slogan: 'Anything, anywhere, anytime—*professionally*'

Above Douglas DC-6, N843TA, at Opa Locka a few weeks before it was due to make a delivery flight to Honduras along with HR-AKW, another Six said to belong to Pan Aviation

Overleaf This anonymous but immaculate Fairchild C-123 Provider was spotted on the perimeter at Opa Locka

Overleaf, inset This head-on shot of the same Provider illustrates the 'wide body' design which made the type such a useful workhorse

It is alleged that this ex-Vortex DC-6, registered N33VX and possibly owned by Universal Air Leasing, is operated by what insiders know as the 'Contra Air Force', which is rumoured to have been involved in the air dropping of military equipment for the Contra rebels in Nicaragua. To avoid the very real threat of being shot down by the Sandinistas, the air drops are thought to have been carried out over Swan Island off the Honduran coast

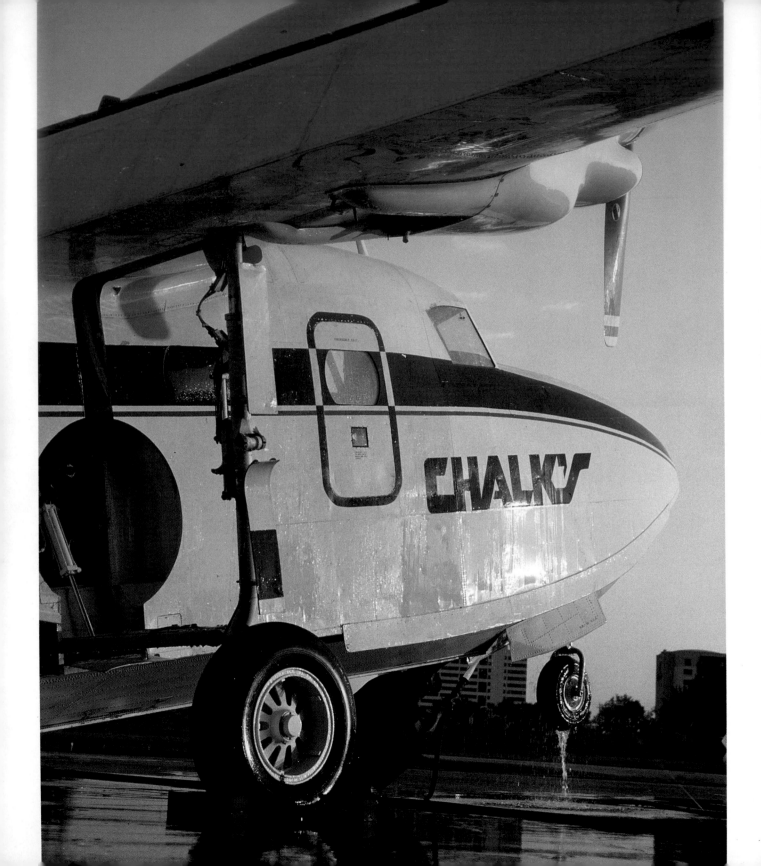

Chalk's

Left A Chalks Turbo Mallard enjoys a giant bird bath as the sun goes down on the ramp at Lauderdale. Each evening the whole fleet returns to be meticulously washed, lubricated and corrosion proofed before operations resume the following day. Sea water and aluminium do not mix well

Below Perched on its tail, this Mallard is drip drying on the far side of the ramp before having its engines washed to remove any salt deposits which may have built up on the turbine blades. To be effective, this task must be performed every day

Overleaf Chalks entire Mallard fleet has now been retrofitted with PT6A turboprop engines. N2969 is undergoing an external visual inspection after being hosed down. The last of Chalks faithful Albatrosses was phased out in early 1988

Preceding pages Water off a duck's back—in this case a Chalks Mallard, getting its feet wet in a growing pool of the cool and clear variety

This page Floodlit by the hangar lights in the fading daylight, it's nearly bedtime for this Mallard

Overleaf An all-action shot of a Mallard landing at Watson Island in downtown Miami, from where you can fly directly to Bimini in the Bahamas. Yes please!

A Mallard climbs out on a westerly heading past a line cruise ships—a constant hazard to seaplanes in this busy port. But the takeoff path at Miami is nowhere near as dramatic as that in St Thomas harbour in the US Virgin Islands

Grounded and impounded

Left Every aircraft in this picture has been impounded by US Customs, and reside here at Hollywood Airport, Fort Lauderdale, awaiting their fate. With all its four props feathered, the KC-97 is unlikely to experience any Florida fun this summer!

This Boeing KC-97, registered N854OD, probably last saw military service with an Air National Guard unit, and since then must have been up to no good before being caught and stored in the Fort Lauderdale Customs' long term parking area

The Cuban owner of this Curtiss C-46, N74173, (parked behind the KC-97) is now a resident of the 'Eglin Hilton', as the Federal Minimum Security Prison is known. His Commando once hauled cargo to the Caribbean islands, as well as specializing in taking loads of furniture to Haiti in exchange for frozen fish

Top left The one that never made it out. It's partner in crime never made it back. C-123 Provider N681DG was said to have left the Davis Monthan boneyard as one of a pair. The other aircraft was allegedly N441OF, the one shot down by the Sandinistas north of San Carlos in Nicaragua in 1986 as it attempted to drop small arms and uniforms to the Contras. In the aftermath of this embarrassing incident, the *Miami Herald* newspaper apparently published a picture which clearly showed an Air America operations manual lying in the wreckage

Left A Douglas A-26 Invader rotting at Opa Locka alongside a C-47 and a DC-6

Above 'Spamcans' are fine, but someday you'll wish you'd flown a real airplane like me!' A DC-3 peers over the fence as a student and his instructor walk out to their Cessna 150 at Opa Locka

A stairway to heaven . . . DC-3 rebuild a Opa Locka. Each nose panel has been painstakingly beaten into shape by hand

These pages This ex-Midway based US Navy C-117 Super Skytrain carries the registration N456WL. It is due to be scrapped, so get your offers in pronto. **Top right** Even closer inspection of the nose reveals this somewhat faded rudy. Must have something to do with the Category of the ILS (Instrument Landing System), but is this Cat 1, Cat 2 or Cat 3?

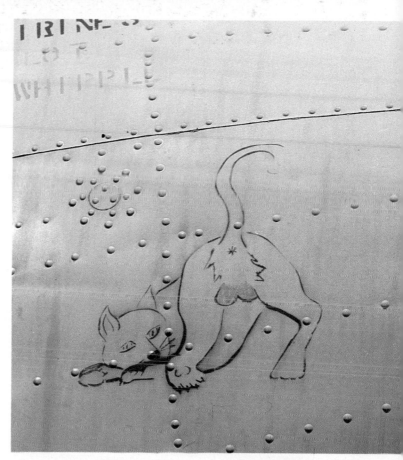

Above Anything but in the pink. A sad end for a classic aircraft, N240BN, the prototype Convair 240, lay awaiting disposal at Opa Locka. Dade County, the owners of the airport, sold the intact Convairliner as scrap for a mere $150 to cut their losses on unpaid parking fees. Shame

Right The Hill Air Company ramp at Ft Lauderdale International is full of interesting specimens. Take C-GGCR, a Douglas DC-3 brought in by some folks who intended to work on it, but who subsequently vanished. As for the Ag Cat, who knows?

Also in the Hill compound, the C-47 (right of picture) is N3753N, an ex-Spanish air force machine owned by Hill. The 'Budget Rent-a-Plane' DC-3, HI445, had recently been gainfully employed in the motion picture *Police Academy 5*

From a distance, the Budget Rent-a-Plane looks a bit of a heap, but closer inspection reveals that all the oil stains are in fact painted on. The airplane is in very good health, having recently received an engine cannibalized from N3753N. In the movie, the DC-3 flies to the Bahamas with three pigs, goats, chickens and 22 toilet seats. Why?

In Florida there were more Connies around than we ever dreamed possible. This L-1049H, registered N1007C, rents space on the Hill ramp, its proud owner working on it weekends. There are clearly a lot of weekends left in it!

The last remnants of what became known as
'Corrosion Corner' at Miami International
following the airport authorities' big tidy up over
the past few years. This DC-7C started life with
Pan Am in 1956 as N741PA. It was re-registered
N74175 around 1965 before being withdrawn
from use in the mid-seventies

Trans-Air-Link's upwardly mobile fleet watches over the sad sight of the DC-7C being chopped up by the blow torch man

Last page With flat tyres all round and generally looking a bit of a mess, Douglas DC-6 N906MA is in a terminal condition at Ft Lauderdale